STRATEGIC TIME

TONY JEARY
THE RESULTS GUY™

RESULTS FASTER!

PUBLISHING

Strategic Time

Published by Results Faster Publishing in association with Clovercroft Publishing, Franklin, Tennessee

Editing by Nonie Jobe and Tawnya Austin

Cover Design by Brooke Hawkins

Interior Design by Adept Content Solutions

Printed in the United States of America

ISBN: 978-1-950892-18-1

BOOKS BY TONY JEARY

Advice Matters

Business Ground Rules

Customer Experience

Family Wealth

High Performing Teams

How to Gain 100 Extra Minutes a Day

Inspire Any Audience

Leadership 25

Let's Start Meeting and Emailing Like This

Leverage

Life is a Series of Presentations

Living in the Black

Mastery

Persuade Any Audience

Presenting with Style

RESULTS Faster

Rich Relationships

Strategic Acceleration

Strategic Eating

Strategic Health

Strategic Preparation

Strategic Time

Success Acceleration

… and dozens more

CONTENTS

A TRIBUTE TO THE GREAT JIM ROHN

One of the most profound thinkers the world ever produced was the late, great Jim Rohn. Nearly two decades ago I connected with Jim and began performing as an MC at his events. Depending on your age and maturity level at any given moment in your life, only select people will have a profound impact on you. Jim and his powerful messages affected me so much that his memory and lessons continue to reverberate throughout my life. I hope this book has that same profound impact on you. To begin, I'd like to share with you a few words Jim spoke about his philosophy on time. I am dedicating this tribute to Jim because it will put you in the right mindset for absorbing the content of this powerful book.

Here's an excerpt from a presentation Jim once shared while discussing time management. We've paraphrased parts of it so we could organize and condense it into his four main points.

Life is not just the passing of time; it is also a collection of experiences. Life is so much more than just watching the clock tick away. It is a collection of experiences characterized by their intensity and frequency.

When my friend Mark died at age forty-four someone said, "That's young to die." But what if Mark managed to squeeze four lifetimes into his brief time here on earth? Mark might not have died so young after all. Whatever the span of your life turns out to be, you must focus on filling your time with experiences and maximizing the intensity of those experiences. I'd like to talk about time management now. The way I see it, there are several ways you can respond when a new subject appears in your life:

1. Ignore the subject. Don't let time management (or anything for that matter) bug you too much because remember, you don't *have* to do anything. Someone might say to you, "I have

to get a handle on my time" The reality is though, you don't have to. If you want to let it all go, you can.

Somebody might also say, "You ought to do this. You should to do that." Here's another point for you to jot down: ignore all the "oughts" or "shoulds." Unless someone is giving general information, the phrase "we should" is much better to use. If you're teaching, then definitely use the phrase "we should," rather than "you should" because the latter is too confrontational. If everyone did this, that would be great. It would let people feel like they're being given an option to choose (without unnecessary tension) rather than being told what to do. Many people easily tend to feel like their personal dignity is being threatened and we don't want to create problems. Remember, don't use "oughts" or "shoulds."

2. Step down to something easier. Imagine a guy in sales who decides he wants to own his company. One day he finally does it, but now he's got no time to play golf. Fed up, he says "When I was in sales, I was making big money and playing golf three days a week. Heck with this owning something! Heck with managing! My life was never my own after I started to manage. I'm going back to sales." See, this is the key…if you're getting too pressed, you might want to consider stepping down. Switch to something with a little less time pressure. If you don't have time for your kids, you especially want to consider slowing down your pace. Remember when I said some things I went for in life ended up costing me too much in the long run? Again, if you're the kind of parent who constantly brings work home and doesn't have time to play with your kids, then I would advise you to step down to something easier.

3. Work longer and harder. However, you must remember that everyone has their limits. I almost lost my health the first year because I went crazy focusing on personal development and achievement. I just went bonkers. I mentioned I was skinny, but by the end of the first year I was a walking shadow. And then it suddenly occurred to me, what if I got rich and was too ill to spend it? This thought was shocking. I used to think,

"If twelve hours won't do it, then I'll work fourteen. If that won't do it, then I'll work eighteen…however long it takes!" Sure enough, this mentality ended up costing me too much.

Working longer and harder might be appropriate in some cases, but not all. If you're just sitting around not doing that much, then working longer and harder might be the right move…you can only work so hard, though. And the key is to not only to work harder, but also work smarter. Do the absolute the best you can in terms of physical output in a reasonable time frame. Working smarter is not only important for improving time management, it will also allow you to become more skillful.

When I first got into sales, I was surrounded by people who were operating with far more efficiency than I was. In order to boost my numbers and compensate for my lack of skill, I worked around the clock. When you're new to the sales industry you can make up in numbers what you lack in skill by working overtime, but this isn't sustainable. When you become more skillful you won't have to pour as much energy into the numbers because your talents and persuasive abilities will guide your sales process. If you work smarter and become more skillful, then time management becomes an easier task.

4. Identify your goals and make detailed plans to accomplish them. You must have clear goals in order to focus your energies and concentrate your talents. You must have detailed step-by-step plans in order to accomplish the activities that guide you towards completing your goal. Next, you must prioritize these activities. It's good use the Pareto Principle (the 80-20 rule) here, which states that 80 percent of the effects come from 20 percent of the causes. For example, if you prepare a list of ten tasks you need to accomplish to achieve a goal, then two of those ten things will be more worth-while.

Being able to determine the most valuable use of your time will set you apart and allow you to achieve above and beyond. Ask yourself, *What is the most valuable use of my time right now?* This is the key question for time management. Also remember to stay with the task that represents the most valuable use of your time, because all other tasks, relatively speaking, are a waste of your time and a waste of your life. All important tasks are difficult, and all unimportant tasks tend to be easy; so be very alert.

Although there's never enough time to do everything that needs to be done, there's always enough time to do the important things. So, focus on those few areas where excellent performance can make an extraordinary difference. Focus on the vital few, versus the trivial many. Concentrate on tasks where you can make a difference with your efforts by honing in on your greatest personal strengths. This is a quality shared by all great leaders; they pick the areas of greatest personal strength, and only take jobs and accept responsibilities where they have the ability and the interest to do an outstanding job.

Focus on areas that align with unique strengths and abilities and delegate everything else to others. Do more of the things that you're better at. Focus on the strengths in the situation, the strengths in other people, and the strengths within your own talents and abilities. Concentrate your resources on the key areas where outstanding results are possible, and continually refer-back to the 80-20 rule. Ask yourself the following questions: *What is the most valuable use of my time? What are my key result areas? What are my vital output areas?* Concentrate always on results, not activities. All peak performers are results oriented.

The wisdom Jim shared about time management resembles what I've been doing for decades now. I don't believe Jim was endorsing the first option—ignoring the subject of time management. Rather, I believe he was simply stating this to help his audience recognize that some people actively choose this option. I believe his second option—stepping down to something easier—might be the best route to take if your actions are not aligned with your values. Over two decades ago I realized I wasn't pouring enough time and energy into my family as I should have been. To remedy this I lowered my goals, shut down my offices, shrank my business, and worked out of my estate for twenty years so I could invest more time in my wife and daughters. Now that my girls have blossomed into prosperous young adults, I have reinvested my allotted family time and built The RESULTS Center.

I've ramped up my own personal time managements effectiveness by doing what Jim suggested in options three and four—continuing to work smarter and make new goals, and then strategically identifying steps to accomplish those goals. Now, I'm currently helping more winners win than ever before.

As you navigate through this brief book, it will become clearer as to why I have chosen to feature Jim Rohn and his powerful words. My goal is to share with you my tips and best practices, and even my perspective on the central theme of this book—*time*. Enjoy and engage with my thoughts and ideas. Use them to teach your team and share them with those in your life who would benefit from improving their time management skills. In other words, share this book with everyone!

INTRODUCTION

I believe you can be strategic about everything, so up to this point I've published:

Strategic Acceleration (my signature book)
Strategic Complaint Resolution
Strategic Eating
Strategic Gifting
Strategic Health
Strategic Network Marketing
Strategic Parenting
Strategic Simplicity
Strategic Willpower
Strategic Wisdom

In this book, we're focusing on being strategic about time, because that's something that can obviously have a dramatic impact on your life, your team, and perhaps your whole organization. Most people waste far too much time, and so do their teams, and that can have a disastrous effect on their organization.

By teaching people all over the world the unique concept we have at the center of our time-management methodology—more *High Leverage Activities* (HLAs) and less *Low Leverage Activities* (LLAs)—we're helping them prioritize their efforts on the things that matter most. Consequently, they're reaping results that many never thought possible.

For years, I've asked audience members around the world to think about how many hours a week they spend in *Low Leverage Activities* (LLAs), and they're shocked when they do. Then I ask how many hours there are in a week, and only 5 percent can answer that without calculating; again, they're shocked.

Then I share my time model (shown below)—168 hours in a week, minus 56 hours for sleeping and 12 hours for maintenance, leaves 100 hours (50 for personal and 50 for professional)—and now I have their full attention.

TONY'S VIEW ON TIME

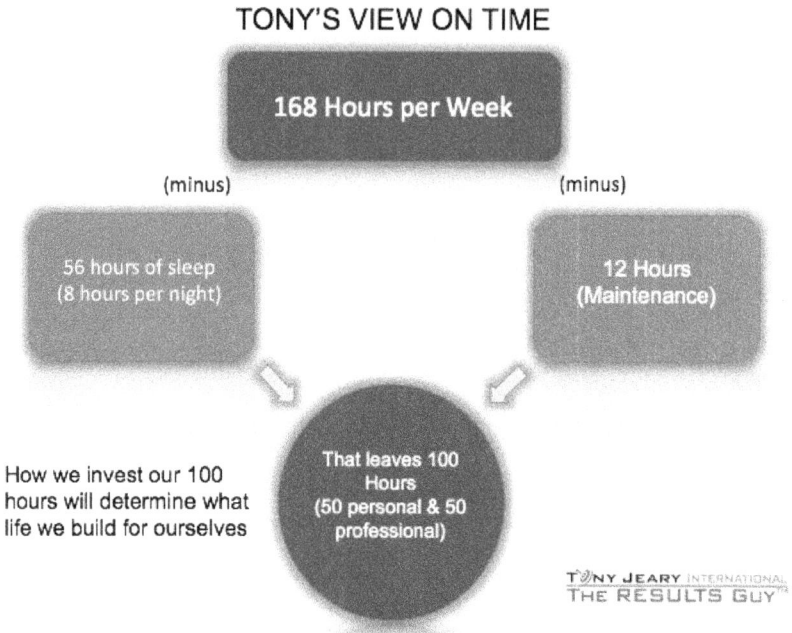

168 Hours per Week

(minus)   (minus)

56 hours of sleep
(8 hours per night)

12 Hours
(Maintenance)

How we invest our 100 hours will determine what life we build for ourselves

That leaves 100 Hours
(50 personal & 50 professional)

TONY JEARY INTERNATIONAL
THE RESULTS GUY

Then I tell them the mistake I made over twenty years ago when I launched my first book on time management, called *How to Gain 100 Extra Minutes a Day*. For years I failed to teach that in order to be really strategic, you need to not just manage your *time*—you need to also manage your *energy*.

Then I tell my audience that of the more than fifty books I've authored (some best sellers, some not), the most impactful thing I've ever come up with (which is also part of my RESULTS Faster methodology) is the concept of *High Leverage Activities* (HLAs). By this time, I've really grabbed them, and hopefully I have also grabbed you.

In the last twenty years since I published *How to Gain 100 Extra Minutes a Day*, we've picked up and developed more time-management tricks, and technology is much more advanced; there's also more of a need for speed. (Do a search for "Tony Jeary, Life Is Fast," and watch this amazing three-minute clip.) So we decided to put this book together to help you be more strategic with your time.

> Here's one of the simple time-management tricks we teach that is an epiphany for many: Most people schedule meetings for one-hour or thirty-minute slots. If you schedule meetings for twenty-five-minute and fifty-minute blocks, you give yourself back an extra ten minutes an hour. Then you have time to go to the bathroom, check your email, and transition to the next meeting, instead of having to go to back-to-back meetings. That's something you may want to integrate into your culture.

Over twenty-five years ago, I developed a global training and consulting organization. My company helped turn around Chrysler in the 1990s, developed Sam Walton's continuation training for Walmart worldwide in the late 1990s, and transformed many of Ford Motor Company's leadership to work together as a high-performing team. During that time, I authored a course/book called *Training Others to Train*, and I became fascinated with the art of training others fast. My fascination has grown since then, and I continue to refine how to compress time in training others. One such way is using my four-step model that defines the layout of this book: Awareness, Skills, Processes, and Tools. We've divided this book into those four main parts that align with my training methodology.

Before we dig into each part, though, there's one more concept I want to share in this introduction. I call it "Level Set":

- We all have the same "level" (amount) of time.
- We can't create more (although we can buy it by hiring others to do things for us).
- Right now, we can't time travel.
- One thing you can do to "set" a new level is create *Elegant Solutions*. *Elegant Solutions* are created when you have such extreme clarity on what you want to accomplish that you can intentionally achieve multiple objectives with a single action or effort. Elegant Solutions can change your life, because they can free up some of your valuable time.

Most people are unaware of their weaknesses when it comes to time management (they have a *Blind Spot*), and those who do often stop improving at the level of great.

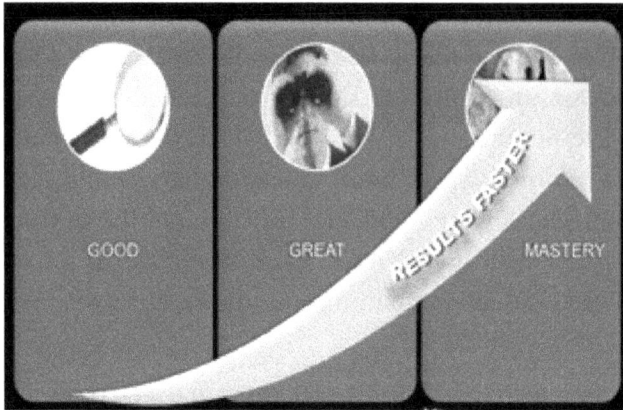

I believe the enemy of mastery is greatness, so I want to take you even higher by showing you how to master these four areas:

Awareness: We'll share such concepts as spending time versus investing time, knowing what you value, the power of sleep, the two types of procrastination, and thinking—perhaps the best use of time (you become what you think about).

Skills (Techniques): We'll show you how to assess your skills, how to say "no" strategically, how to have great meetings, how to use your phone strategically, and how to strengthen your delegation and organizational skills.

Processes: We'll cover high-impact strategies such as simple daily-list management, team huddles, putting things on automatic, creating morning and evening rituals, and asking yourself often during the day, *What's the best use of my time right now?*

Tools: We'll teach you more about saving time by using your phone and lists strategically, and we'll share one of our most impactful templates—our Accelerator Matrix—to help you identify your HLAs and the roadblocks you'll need to bust to achieve them. Then we'll highlight a time-management tool many people miss—standards. And finally, I'll share with you select ideas from our goal-setting toolbox.

What I aim to do every day is positively impact people. That's the way I measure my life, and I'm so blessed to be able to do so! I hope you've already experienced an epiphany or two in this introduction that will impact your life. Get ready for many more!

CHAPTER ONE
AWARENESS

Awareness is the first step in our time-management model, because there are certain foundational distinctions you need to be aware of before you can effectively utilize the skills, processes, and tools we'll give you later.

Spending Versus Investing—Own Your Time

Are you spending your time or investing it?

Most people use the word "spend" when they talk about the way they use their time. They don't realize they're unconsciously putting a negative trajectory into their vocabulary, mind, and actions. The better word, in my opinion, is the word "invest," because it implies that you own your own time, and it's up to you how you use it.

This concept is an epiphany for many people; they've never really thought about the difference. *Spending* your time is akin to wasting it (spinning your wheels, if you will). When you own your own time, you intentionally *invest* it—whether you work for someone, you're an entrepreneur, or you run the whole show.

We hope a big win from this book are the epiphanies you may have never thought about, such as:

- There are 168 hours in a week, and you have approximately 100 hours to invest in your professional life and in your personal life.
- Most people waste about twenty hours a week in LLAs (*Low Leverage Activities*).
- You may be *spending* time rather than *investing* it.

Here's an example: In my company, Tony Jeary International, we like to live by the philosophies we teach. One of those is that, at the beginning of each day, we *invest* time going over the master to-do list. Do we enjoy it? Not really, because it can be a boring, mundane task. But (and I don't use the word "but" often, unless it's extremely intentional) what it does is reinforce the clarity of what we accomplished or didn't get accomplished the day before. In other words, it forces accountability. If we see that something has been on the list for three days, it's obviously not getting executed, and we can take action accordingly. Consequently, it's an important *investment* of our time. We process a ton of projects/tasks to help support our clients at the same time; and we work very quickly, because our clients expect speedy results. It's critical that we catch everything we should be doing, and this practice keeps things from falling through the cracks.

We teach and use a concept called "putting an X in the box" on our to-do list. The X, of course, signifies that the task has been accomplished. Here's the catch: when we FedEx something to someone, we don't get a whole X; we get a slash. Sending it is just part of the task. When the person *receives* it, that's when we get to put an X in the box. When we send something back for a refund, we don't get a full X in the box until the refund is received. We teach and live total completion.

Know What You Value—Everything Ties Back to It

In just about every book I author, I mention the importance of knowing your values. If you don't know what you value, you can't set goals and take actions that will be congruent with what you really want in life. We've developed a tool called a Values Matrix (which we share below) that can help you build your goals tied to your values. First, though, you'll need to identify your top values (ten or so) from the list we've provided here:

1. Affection	21. Friendship	41. Personal Brand
2. Alignment	22. Fun	42. Personal Improvement
3. Altruism	23. Generosity	43. Personal Salvation
4. Appearance	24. Genuineness	44. Philanthropy
5. Appreciated	25. Happiness	45. Power
6. Attitude	26. Harmony	46. Productivity
7. Cleanliness	27. Health	47. Recognition
8. Congruence	28. Honesty	48. Respect
9. Contentment	29. Humility	49. Results
10. Cooperation	30. Inner Peace	50. Romance
11. Creativity	31. Inspiration	51. Routine
12. Education	32. Intimacy	52. Security
13. Effectiveness	33. Joy	53. See the World
14. Efficiency	34. Knowledge	54. Simplicity
15. Fairness	35. Lifestyle	55. Solitude
16. Faith	36. Loved	56. Spiritual Maturity
17. Fame	37. Loyalty	57. Status
18. Family	38. Motivation	58. Wealth
19. Financial Security	39. Openness	59. Winning
20. Freedom	40. Organization	60. Wisdom

Now, in the Values Matrix below, write your top values in the column on the left:

VALUES GOALS MATRIX

#	Values	Personal HLA's	Professional HLA's	Personal Goals	Professional Goals
1.					
2.					
3.					
4.					
5.					
6.					
7.					
8.					
9.					
10.					

Goals: F=Finance P=Physical H=Home Life E=Education S=Social SP=Spiritual

Now, identify your HLAs that support your personal and professional goals, making sure they align with the values you listed. Those HLAs are where you should invest your time. [Note: HLA stands for High Leverage Activity, so it is an activity.]

THE HLAS THAT ALIGN WITH YOUR VALUES AND SUPPORT YOUR PERSONAL AND PROFESSIONAL GOALS ARE WHERE YOU SHOULD INVEST YOUR TIME.

One of the things we value is increasing the profits of our clients. So one of our HLAs would be to listen to our clients so we'll know what's important to them (their goals). Sometimes what's important to them is trajectory. They might be willing to give up smaller profits now to have their business grow in a certain direction. Or selling their business several years down the line may be what's important to them. And people buy a business for more reasons than just money; they may buy for trajectory or for brand, or maybe for the database. We would need to invest our time (HLAs) toward increasing all those assets in order to optimize their potential sale.

If some people say they really value their health, we would have to test them and ask, "How much time and money did you invest (not spend) in your health and in improving yourself last year?" If that number is low, then maybe they don't really value their health the way they say they do. (That's an example of how you can check to make sure you're investing your time in a manner that aligns with your values.)

If a client comes in and says, "I value my family," I would say, "Great! How much time do you invest in appreciating your kids?" If the client responds, "Well, not enough!" I would have to say, "Okay, if you truly value your family, then you need to make an effort to appreciate them more. If family is one of your values, then you certainly need to invest time in your family to make sure you're pouring into them."

168—It's All We Have

Time is an equalizer. We all have the same amount of time. No one has enough, and yet everyone has all there is.

Time is extremely valuable. Remember the time model we served up in the introduction? We all have 168 hours in a week, and if we subtract 56 hours for sleep (8 hours a night) and 12 hours for maintenance, that leaves 100 hours, 50 to invest personally and 50 to invest professionally. How we invest those hours (how well we focus on our HLAs) in both areas will determine the life we build for ourselves. It can make the difference between winning and losing. Lack of clarity on your HLAs will lead to poor time management and will put you in a position where you're often saying "yes" to the wrong things and not living the life you really want to live.

When launching my book *Life Is a Series of Presentations* in 2004, I decided to publish it with Simon & Schuster. Several years earlier that same company had published *Unlimited Power* by Tony Robbins and *The 7 Habits of Highly Successful People* by Steven R. Covey, so I thought, *I need to study this publisher.* I reached out to Covey's partner Greg Link and was able to engage Covey to show me how to work with Simon & Schuster to get similar results. Greg and I, as well as Steven M. Covey (Steven R.'s son) have become great friends and business colleagues since

> HOW WE INVEST THE 50 HOURS (HOW WELL WE FOCUS ON OUR HLAS) IN BOTH THE PERSONAL AND THE PROFESSIONAL AREAS OF OUR LIFE WILL DETERMINE THE LIFE WE BUILD FOR OURSELVES.

then. (As a spinoff from *The 7 Habits*, Greg and Steven M. created two powerful books that I recommend you read: *The Speed of Trust* and *Smart Trust.* Both books are helping individuals and organizations all over the world achieve prosperity from high-trust relationships and cultures.) In *The 7 Habits*, Steven came up with a powerful model that imparted to the world the importance of managing your time, and our HLA model overlays nicely on his. (See below.)

Stephen Covey's Time Management Matrix		
High Leverage Activities	URGENT	NOT URGENT
Important	QUADRANT 1 Crises High-Impact Deadlines Pressing Problems	Quadrant 2 Being Organized Building Relationships Planning Exercise and Recreation
Not Important	Quadrant 3 Interruptions Some Phone Calls Some E-Mail	Quadrant 4 Busy Work Some Phone Calls Some E-Mail Time Wasters — **Low Leverage Activities**

Quadrant 1 (urgent/important) is where most people want to stay to ensure they're investing their time (HLAs) in what's most important and what matters the most now.

Quadrant 4 (not urgent/not important) is where you don't want to spend time—on busy work and unimportant or lengthy phone calls and emails (LLAs).

Power of Sleep (56 Hours Well Invested)

The need for adequate sleep was a *Blind Spot* for me for years. Until just a few years ago, I made the mistake of believing that motivated people like myself could carve time out of our sleep to take more action. However, I discovered that you sacrifice some things when you lose too much sleep, including:

- Being able to operate and think at peak performance
- Allowing your system (your body) to reset so your hormones can operate at the optimum level

Few things have a greater consistent impact on your daily performance and well-being than a good night's sleep. New research reveals that adequate sleep is directly related to the ability to avoid acute and chronic diseases. Everything—from weight gain and the ability to fight off the common cold to the risk for high blood pressure, coronary artery disease, diabetes, and chronic inflammation—is greatly affected by quality of sleep. And current science shows you should have six to seven forty- to sixty-minute REM cycles. (See my book *Strategic Health*; one sixth of that book has to do with sleep.)

FEW THINGS HAVE A GREATER CONSISTENT IMPACT ON YOUR DAILY PERFORMANCE AND WELL-BEING THAN A GOOD NIGHT'S SLEEP.

You can see how allocating time to sleeping well links into investing your time. If you aren't getting proper sleep, you're likely at increased risk of disease and may not be functioning at your optimal level in many aspects of your life.

The Mind (Beta/Alpha/Delta)

I believe this one will be a huge "aha" for many people.

Before my good friend Dr. Kevin Light passed away in 2018, we were coauthoring a book together called *Win More: The Science of Goal Achievement*. In the book, we talked about three areas you must manage well if you want to see the best results toward achieving your goals—the brain, the mind, and the body. In the brain realm you must master four areas: habit management, your reticular activating system (your RAS, which controls what the brain lets in and absorbs), your brain waves, and of course, knowledge. All four areas link to time management; however, I want to focus for a moment on brain waves.

Have you ever been wrestling to remember something or solve a problem, and the memory or the solution suddenly comes to you when you're first coming out of a deep sleep in the morning? That's because, as you're waking up in the morning and coming out of a deep relaxation, your brain is in a frequency called alpha, which is the gateway to your subconscious mind.

AS YOU'RE WAKING UP IN THE MORNING AND COMING OUT OF A DEEP RELAXATION, YOUR BRAIN IS IN A FREQUENCY CALLED ALPHA, WHICH IS THE GATEWAY TO YOUR SUBCONSCIOUS MIND.

BRAIN MANAGEMENT

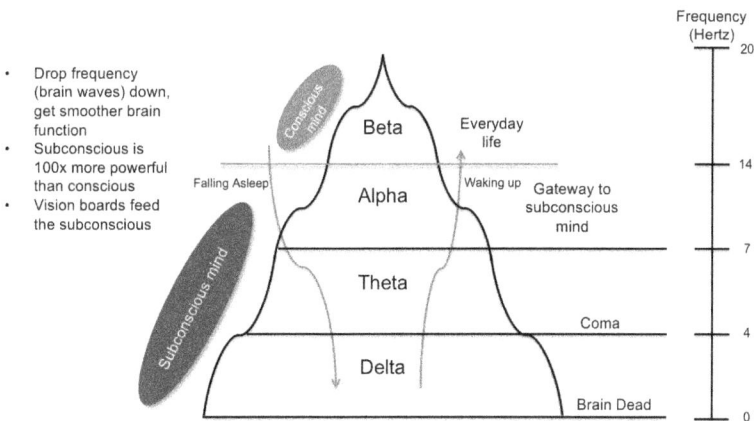

- Drop frequency (brain waves) down, get smoother brain function
- Subconscious is 100x more powerful than conscious
- Vision boards feed the subconscious

Conscious mind

Subconscious mind

Beta — Everyday life

Falling Asleep

Alpha — Waking up — Gateway to subconscious mind

Theta

Coma

Delta

Brain Dead

Frequency (Hertz)
20
14
7
4
0

When we're awake and going through daily life, we're at about a seventeen on the brain-wave frequency scale and in Beta operation mode. On the other end, we're at about a three or four when we're in a coma, and when we die, we're at the Delta stage. So we go back and forth between Beta and Alpha in our daily twenty-four-hour cycle.

Alpha is a relaxed, yet focused, state of mind that allows you to be more receptive, open, and creative. When we utilize the alpha state, we have better memory and recall. Learning to access alpha at will can help sharpen your intuition; and if used on a regular basis—even for short periods—it can help you more easily cope with stress and reduce anxiety. And because you are calmer, you tend to be more prepared—you're more focused, make better decisions, and come to solutions faster.

Now let's link that to time management. If you'll intentionally invest a few extra minutes to stay in bed and let your brain wake up slowly, it will often think about challenges you need to solve or things you need to remember. It could be the answer to a problem you've been struggling with, something you've been trying to remember, or even a new idea to help you up your game. Whatever it is, you've just invested a few minutes of your valuable time to come up with something that may have taken hours, days, or even weeks to discover otherwise. If you'll have the discipline to get up immediately and write it down, you can be more efficient with the way you manage your time.

> IF YOU'LL INTENTIONALLY INVEST A FEW EXTRA MINUTES TO STAY IN BED AND LET YOUR BRAIN WAKE UP SLOWLY, IT WILL OFTEN THINK ABOUT CHALLENGES YOU NEED TO SOLVE OR THINGS YOU NEED TO REMEMBER.

Thinking—Perhaps the Best Use of Time

High achievers want results. They want to win, and they're often faced with problems. One of those problems is that they want results faster. That may be what you're facing, as well. I believe every problem is a thinking problem. So what do you do when you don't get the results you want or when you don't get the results you want fast enough? You make some changes! You use intentional thinking to look at all the pieces and make strategic decisions. That means you have to let go of old thought patterns and be open to new ways of thinking.

Our world changes daily, and it doesn't take long for knowledge to become outdated, for skills to weaken, or for paradigms to shift. Unless you're willing to, as Abraham Lincoln once said, "think anew and act anew," you're likely to make very poor choices. You have to constantly check your thinking to make sure it hasn't become outdated.

How you think affects what you can or can't accomplish. Earl Nightingale recorded and later wrote *The Strangest Secret*, considered one of the greatest motivational books of all time. What was his "strangest secret"? **You become what you think about**. Nightingale claimed that only 5 percent of the people in the world achieve success, simply because of the way they think. People who set goals succeed because they know where they are going. They have planted their goals in their mind.

How does this link to time management? Thinking matters much more than people believe it does. Many just keep working away at their to-do list, versus really thinking about the right things they should be doing.

I've been coaching and working with my good friend Kevin Guest, the CEO of a wonderful public company called USANA, for almost a decade and a half, and I just helped him launch a powerful book called *All the Right Reasons*.

One of the really cool things about Kevin is that he continually encourages me to make "thinking" an HLA for every one of his executives I coach. He wants me to teach them to put thinking time on their calendars, because he says it's one of the best uses of his executives' time and it's what will take them to another level. Well, it's been working great. In the first year and a half after we started that, the company's market capitalization went up over 30 percent—by $500 million dollars—and his organization recently hit the $1 billion mark!

One of my tag lines is "Change your thinking, change your results." Decide now what you want and plant that goal in your mind. Then be *Intentionally Strategic* (cast deliberate and calculated thinking toward your purpose, your goals, and your objectives) about everything you do, and that will lead to the results you're looking for.

Procrastination (Positive and Negative)

When we launched *Strategic Acceleration,* I introduced the concept of positive and negative procrastination. I've since gone on to do a CBS special on the concept. (Do a search for "Tony Jeary on procrastination" to watch this powerful three-minute video.)

CHANGE YOUR THINKING, CHANGE YOUR RESULTS. DECIDE NOW WHAT YOU WANT AND PLANT THAT GOAL IN YOUR MIND. THEN BE *INTENTIONALLY STRATEGIC* ABOUT EVERYTHING YOU DO, AND THAT WILL LEAD TO THE RESULTS YOU'RE LOOKING FOR.

Think about your self-talk right now. Is it supporting you and giving you legitimate reasons to put things off, or not? You see, all procrastination comes back to self-talk— what you say to yourself. Sometimes, we say things like, *Oh, it doesn't really matter. I'll do that later. No one cares.* Or sometimes we may say, *You know, I just don't feel like doing that right now.* That's negative procrastination.

A legitimate thing to say to ourselves, when it's true, may be, *I need to take a little bit of time to gain some more valuable insights before I make that decision.* That's positive procrastination. Even if you say, *I need to sleep on it tonight,* because you know you'll make a better decision if you let your intuition work throughout the evening and night, that's positive procrastination.

Generally speaking, though, negative procrastination is putting things off when you shouldn't. To gain results, you need to take charge of your time and your life. Here are a few examples of possible ways to contradict negative self-talk.

- *I can do it tomorrow.* Ask, *What can I get started on now that will help me complete this project and help the others who are waiting for me?*
- *I don't have everything I need, so I'll wait.* Ask, *What can I do now, with what I have on hand?*
- *I can't do it perfectly* (or, *I need to do more research*), *so I'll wait.* Practice *Production Before Perfection* (PBP), which may be the most

important of all my time-management concepts. It's the principle that says you must not allow the fear of lack of perfectionism stop you from starting. It's often best to jump in and make things happen first, and then you can perfect as you go.

- *I don't have time right now.* Ask, *What can I do in the next five (ten, fifteen, twenty) minutes that will move me toward the results I want?*
- *Someone else can do it better.* Say to yourself, *Even if someone else can do this better, it's my task and my responsibility. I may even get better as I keep working on this!*
- *I just don't feel like it right now.* Many people find that getting started is the biggest hurdle. Say to yourself, *I'll just do five (ten, fifteen, twenty) minutes of work on this.* You'll see that you often get caught up in the task and make tremendous progress.

Remember, it's only when you start doing what you need to do that you can begin to produce results. Waiting and *Strategic Acceleration* are not compatible. If you do nothing, that's exactly what you'll get—nothing. If you do something, the possibilities are endless. Be like Nike—do it now!

GENERALLY SPEAKING, NEGATIVE PROCRASTINATION IS PUTTING THINGS OFF WHEN YOU SHOULDN'T. TO GAIN RESULTS, YOU NEED TO TAKE CHARGE OF YOUR TIME AND YOUR LIFE. WAITING AND *STRATEGIC ACCELERATION* ARE NOT COMPATIBLE. IF YOU DO NOTHING, THAT'S EXACTLY WHAT YOU'LL GET— NOTHING. IF YOU DO SOMETHING, THE POSSIBILITIES ARE ENDLESS.

Chapter Two
Skills

The second part of our time-management model is Skills. Few people are natural at effective time management. Most have to master a set of skills that will teach them how to properly think about and invest their time so they can get the best possible results in life. I've loved teaching these skills to my clients over the years and then watching their results soar once they master them—along with the processes and tools we'll cover in chapters three and four, of course.

The Assessment

First, before we get into the skills, we would like you to evaluate where you are in your ability to manage time, and that could include a variety of things. For example:

- What's your skill set on communicating approval for someone to be on your calendar?
- What's your skill set to be able to give people what they want and yet say "no" to what they're actually requesting?
- How are you doing in the area of delegation?

Many people don't want to take a frank look at their time-management skills, because they know they're lacking in this department. And yet confronting your weaknesses head-on is a required first step if you want to go from Point A to Point B. You must look at yourself in the mirror and ask, *Is that an area of weakness I need to work on?*

We've developed several tools over the years to help you assess where you are in the area of time management. Let's start with four helpful audits from my original book on time management, *How to Gain 100 Extra Minutes a Day*, which we've updated to today's standards. As you go through each of the four audits—on prioritization, procrastination, organization,

YOU MUST LOOK AT YOURSELF IN THE MIRROR AND ASK, *IS THAT AN AREA OF WEAKNESS I NEED TO WORK ON?*

and delegation—estimate in the column on the far right how many minutes you could save or gain by following the suggestion, or following it better.

PRIORITIZATION TIME GAINERS' AUDIT

	Event	Gained Minutes
❑	Set priorities during daily planning, eliminating unproductive tasks, to gain valuable time.	_____
❑	Have a written agenda for every meeting, with no more than three objectives, and follow it.	_____
❑	Learn to say "no" to demands that don't benefit you, or send the request to the appropriate person.	_____
❑	Learn when your high-energy time is and schedule your priority work for this time.	_____
❑	Prioritize your reading by learning to skim articles, memos, books, etc. Then read only what really gives you value.	_____
❑	Request that people who send you emails prioritize and spell out the actions they're asking of you in clear bullet points, rather than long narratives.	_____
❑	Write down your objectives before you return phone calls to gain time through quicker, more effective communication.	_____
❑	Early in the day, sort mail and place each piece appropriately (now, future, trash) to gain valuable time throughout the day, as each piece is addressed only once.	_____
❑	Ask the originator of a document to send you only the relevant information that pertains to you.	_____
❑	Create lists often to help with focus and multitasking.	_____
❑	Prioritize and review the list of tasks you have given a subordinate.	_____
❑	Gain time by having visitors screened, and only meet with those you must. Stand when you greet drop-ins to shorten the visit.	_____
❑	Use a to-do list on your phone to help prioritize daily events.	_____
❑	Control time-wasting activities.	_____
❑	Other _____	_____
	Total Time Gained	_____

PROCRASTINATION TIME GAINERS' AUDIT

	Event	Gained Minutes
❑	Getting up "X" amount of minutes earlier every day can give you more productive time.	_____
❑	Identifying and doing "little" things when you have open minutes while waiting will gain you extra minutes later, because they will already be completed.	_____
❑	Making "to-do" lists and marking items off as they are accomplished earns you valuable time later, as you gain confidence and satisfaction in seeing things accomplished. This reduces possible procrastination.	_____
❑	Identifying deadlines every morning gains time and hinders procrastination.	_____
❑	Identify frequent tasks that you have previously procrastinated on and perform them way out in advance.	_____
❑	Gain valuable minutes by starting the day's tasks quickly; do not ponder the difficulties of the day. Lay out your first job the night before.	_____
❑	Break one big task for this week (or month) into smaller, manageable parts to help fight the tendency to procrastinate.	_____
❑	Stocking up on all supplies (greeting cards, birthday cards, stamps, gifts, etc.) gains extra minutes by not having to go shopping for them individually.	_____
❑	Once an assignment has reached the "emergency" level, it has been procrastinated on. Identify future assignments and gain valuable time by listing the tasks needed to assure they won't become emergencies.	_____
❑	Preprinting postcards and labels for repetitive correspondence gains critical time every time you send one. Think about using macros and form letters on your computer.	_____
❑	Other _____	_____
❑	Other _____	_____
❑	Other _____	_____
	Total Time Gained	_____

Organization Time Gainers' Audit

	Event	Gained Minutes
❏	Purchase a postage meter and keep stamps on hand, or print your own, to save trips to the post office.	_____
❏	Double up on tasks (exercise + reading = savings).	_____
❏	Listen to audio books while you drive—great for research.	_____
❏	Store things close to where they are used (paper, supplies, etc.) to save walking from one place to another.	_____
❏	Designate a special shelf or area where you put items for repair, and work on one when you have a few spare minutes.	_____
❏	Use a color-coded filing system so you can find important papers and documents faster.	_____
❏	Keep a project by the phone to work on while talking.	_____
❏	Combine errands to gain time and increase productivity. Take a list with you.	_____
❏	Develop a "template" agenda (for example, the 3-D Outline™ format taught in my book *Inspire Any Audience*) for meetings, and fine-tune it for every meeting.	_____
❏	Keep materials with you to read while you are waiting in line, getting your car repaired, etc.	_____
❏	Use a headset when making calls so you can simultaneously work on other things (not always practical—be sure it does not detract from the call).	_____
❏	Provide guidelines for screening incoming mail to keep the trivial mail away from you (if applicable).	_____
❏	Use the forward and delete keys often when processing email.	_____
❏	Use prepackaged kits for overnight travel. This will gain you the time it takes to pack these items each time.	_____
❏	Use a checklist for travel items, and keep it inside your suitcase to save time when packing.	_____
❏	Keep extra stamps in your wallet.	_____
	Total Time Gained	_____

DELEGATION TIME GAINERS' AUDIT

Event	Gained Minutes
☐ Trade projects with an associate whose abilities and gifts fit the project better than yours.	_____
☐ Plan a follow-up meeting with someone you've delegated to and check the status of the item or event delegated. This time spent will gain you time later, as the project is completed on time.	_____
☐ Utilize administrative personnel to handle correspondence, filings, mailing, etc.	_____
☐ Use delivery (courier) and cleaning services to free up your time to do what you do best. "Trade money for time."	_____
☐ Make a daily list of items that need to be performed, and rate them from 1 to 10 on how they fit your HLAs. Work only on those items that rate above a seven. Delegate all others to gain valuable time.	_____
☐ Contract outside services or consultants when no one in-house has the skills to perform the task or all staff is overburdened. This will gain you valuable time by not having to train and retrain someone.	_____
☐ Give enough detailed feedback on projects so the recipients can learn and increase their skills for the next project. This will gain you time in redos.	_____
☐ By delegating someone to extract the key points from long reports, you will gain time, as well as pertinent information, for faster, more effective results.	_____
☐ Have others read for you and summarize key points.	_____
☐ Use Post-It Notes™ effectively to delegate to others. A quick note can save valuable time if both people are not together for the handoff.	_____
☐ Record assignments on your phone if you don't write well or have a driving trip where you can delegate.	_____
☐ Other _____	_____
☐ Other _____	_____
☐ Other _____	_____
☐ Other _____	_____
☐ Other _____	_____
Total Time Gained	_____

The Time Savers' Audit below is another tool we've developed more recently to help you assess areas where you could and should be saving time. Rate yourself (1 to 4) on each item to see where you stand.

TIME SAVERS' AUDIT

#	Time Saving Idea	Notes and Examples	Action	Rating
		Conserve		**(1-4)**
1.	Don't Overdo	• Don't put unnecessary effort into a project/task.		
2.	Book Meetings to Maximize Time	• Book for 25- and 50-minute windows vs. 30 and 60 to allow transition time.		
3.	Know Objectives of Each Meeting	• Have your team review your calendar 3 days out and help you prepare. • Get selected people to presend info to help both you and them prep to help shorten each call or meeting.		
		Thinking		**(1-4)**
4.	Identify Your High-Energy Time	• Schedule your priority, high-impact activities for this time… for better and faster results.		
5.	Have Staff Know Calendar & Send	• Have staff send an email the previous night with the next day's calendar.		
6.	Assess Your Self-Talk	• Change self-talk, if needed. • Speak into action (i.e., who you are, how are you going to do each presentation, call, life, etc.) • Say things like, "I am on time and often finish early."		

#	Time Saving Idea	Notes and Examples	Action	Rating
		Planning Ahead		**(1-4)**
7.	Build a Stronger Resource Library	• Capture best practices (presentation prep, hiring, coaching, assessing, etc.).		
8.	Give Enough Detail and Feedback	• Train for the future. • This will gain you time over and over in future assignments.		
9.	Make Planning an HLA	• Carve out even more planning time.		
10.	Live *Elegant Solutions*	• Intentionally create situations where you are accomplishing multiple things at once.		
		Utilize Team Better		**(1-4)**
11.	Show Appreci-ation	• When team members save you time, show appreciation and recognize them.		
12.	Provide Op-portunities for Improvement	• Encourage direct reports to take professionally applicable classes.		
13.	Communicate Regular Feed-back	• Recognize efforts and offer areas of improvement.		
14.	Take Live Notes (Using Team)	• Have assistant listen in on calls and take notes to organize faster.		
15.	Read *A Message to Garcia*	• Have direct reports read and study.		
		Setup		**(1-4)**
16.	Allocate Time Limit for Each Task	• As a habit, have time limits for meetings, calls, emails, etc.		
17.	Think through Objectives	• Take a few seconds to think through your objectives when you return calls.		
18.	Confirm Others' Available Time	• At the beginning of the call, confirm the amount of time others have available.		

#	Time Saving Idea	Notes and Examples	Action	Rating
		Delegate		**(1-4)**
19.	Contract Outside Services	• Reason to contract outside services and consultants: no one in-house has the skills, not enough capacity to perform the task, etc.		
20.	Present Headline First	• When your people communicate with you, have them present the headline first (send initial emails or call first).		
21.	Read with Intentionality	• Skim articles, books, and memos. • Have reports highlighted in your style.		
22.	Create Custom Tools	• Types of tools: templates, reports, forms, etc. • Name them specific to the task.		
23.	Share Shortcuts & Best Practices	• Share the most efficient ways to get things done that align with your needs. • Keep things off your plate.		
		Meetings		**(1-4)**
24.	Have Meetings Start without You	• When possible, have meetings start without you. • When you arrive, get a summary.		
25.	Use Web Meetings	• Leverage communication methods. • Have staff become exceptional at setup and support of web meetings.		

Total: _____

Saying "No" Strategically

Are you saying "no" enough? In my opinion, that's the most important word there is in regard to time management, and hence productivity and results!

Saying "no" is an overlooked secret to success. In today's fast-paced world, we're presented with opportunities almost every waking minute. There are commercials, messages, products, emails, phone calls, offers, meetings, and activities of all kinds bombarding us from all sides, and most people don't know how to deal with them effectively. Saying "no" can be like magic in impacting your time effectiveness; it takes discipline and good thinking to a whole new level.

Saying "no" is important, yet it doesn't have to be a negative. Let me give you an example. Let's say Roland calls and says, "Hey, Tony, I was wondering if we could have lunch." I think, *Hmmm. Is having lunch with Roland an HLA or not? Well, maybe not.* So I say, "What's up?" and Roland says, "Well, you know John, and I would like to meet John. I'd like to have lunch and talk about your making that connection." So I say, "Roland, how about this? I can just send you both an email to introduce you to each other, and you guys can be instantly connected. What do you think?" He says, "Great! I didn't really have time to have lunch with you, anyway! I just wanted to meet John." I was able to give Roland what he wanted in a matter of seconds instead of burning two hours for lunch.

> SAYING "NO" IS AN OVERLOOKED SECRET TO SUCCESS.

People want to have lunch with me all the time, or they want to have a phone call or a meeting. Often, before I say "yes," I'll say, "How about this? Let's start with a ten- or fifteen-minute phone call."

Learning when and how to say "no" is one of the most valuable lessons of leadership. Here are a few tips:

- "No" does not have to be a negative. Saying "no" respectfully can be well received, and it will help you to own your life again.
- The first person we must learn to say "no" to is ourselves. We must say "no" to activities we would prefer to engage in, and "yes" to what we actually need to do.
- Most often, the right time to say "no" is at the beginning. It's much harder to get yourself out of a commitment than to not make the commitment at all.
- Don't be afraid to say "no" to *Low Leverage Activities*, even if you've been doing them for a while, so you can put more time toward your HLAs.

- Part of successfully saying "no" is about the intent behind it. Done properly, people will understand that you are saying "no" because their request doesn't fit into your strategic priorities. Your intent is to free yourself up to better prioritize your time to focus on your HLAs.
- Sometimes saying "no" actually means saying "not now." For example, you may need to defer a meeting or a conversation until you've finished with other priorities.
- There are many ways to say "no" and still make people feel you care. You can say "no" to your child's request for an expensive gadget, for instance, and instead spend time teaching him or her a new sport or game. If you get invited to participate in a project that will pull you away from your HLAs, you can say "no" and suggest someone else for the job, or give the project leader ideas and suggestions for getting things rolling.

The most important tip for saying "no" smartly is to make a habit of evaluating everything according to your HLAs.

THE MOST IMPORTANT TIP FOR SAYING "NO" SMARTLY IS TO MAKE A HABIT OF EVALUATING EVERYTHING ACCORDING TO YOUR HLAs.

THE *PREPARATION* AND THE *FOLLOW-UP* ARE OFTEN AS IMPORTANT AS THE DELIVERY FOR ACHIEVING YOUR MEETING OBJECTIVES.

Meetings

When you think about saving time in relation to meetings, you probably, like most people, think about saving time within the meeting. Right? Actually, the preparation and the follow-up are often equally important for achieving your meeting objectives. Proper preparation may save you from the necessity of having two or three additional meetings, and, by following up correctly, you may be able to save a ton of time in execution.

Several years ago, I coauthored a book with my good friend George Lowe, called *We've Got to Start Meeting and Emailing Like This.*

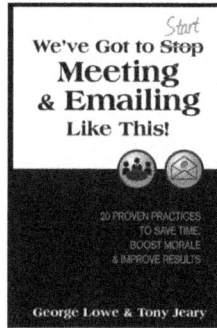

A powerful takeaway from that book is the list of standards we recommend for having great meetings, which include constructive actions for preparation, delivery, and follow-up. We suggest you let your meeting attendees know what to expect through these written standards:

1. Have a clear purpose and defined objective(s).

2. Ensure that the right people are either in the room, on the phone, or represented.

3. Create *and follow* a realistic, timed agenda.

4. Start and end meetings on time.

5. Acknowledge that achieving winning outcomes is not just the meeting leader's responsibility—it's everyone's responsibility.

6. Facilitate for results so everyone stays involved and engaged.

7. Take thorough notes. Develop a "who-does-what-by-when" action plan.

8. Align meetings at twenty-five- and fifty-minute increments instead of thirty and sixty.

9. Publish meeting notes and action plans quickly, and follow up to ensure timely execution.

10. Strategically cascade meeting outcomes promptly and consistently to others in the organization.

Prioritization

Here are nine keys to help you master the skill of prioritization:

1. Set priorities aligned with your predetermined HLAs and review them throughout the day. Eliminating unproductive tasks keeps you focused on the right things. Prioritize your list, using your HLAs as headers.

> Another exceptional idea is to assign written HLAs to each position on your team, rather than just a job description. This can save you time in management, and it will also help your team be more productive.

2. Have strong written agendas tied to clear objectives for every meeting you attend, lead, or grant.

3. Identify your high-energy times, and schedule your priority high-impact activities to coincide with them.

4. Learn to say "no" more often to demands that don't fit and support your highest priorities (as we discussed earlier).

5. Leverage your reading and study by skimming articles, memos, reports, and even books. Commission team members or other colleagues to read and summarize for you.

6. Ask the people who send you regular emails to prioritize and spell out the actions they're asking of you with clear bullet points, rather than long narratives.

7. Write down or think through your objectives before you make phone calls. This will also help you leave better *action-oriented* voicemail.

8. Ask the originators who send you emails, texts, voicemail, or any other type of communication to send you only relevant information that pertains to you.

9. Create and leverage lists often. Then ask yourself several times every day, *What's the best use of my time right now?* This is one of my favorite and most powerful time-management secrets.

The most successful people don't dwell on problems; they live in solutions. We know that change happens fast and often without warning, and that problems do exist. Often our natural inclination is to develop a quick tactical response to a perceived problem, when we actually need to react strategically. (Being tactical involves doing things like tasks, calls, activities, and paperwork. Being strategic involves things like planning, thinking, and studying.) *Strategic IQ* is about balancing that out. Sometimes you'll need to prioritize on the tactical side, and sometimes you'll need to prioritize on the strategic side. In either case, you need to ask yourself, *What's the best use of my time right now?* ten, fifteen, or twenty times a day. Then you'll be able to zero in on your high-priority actions as you look at your list(s) of all the things you want to get done. (We'll talk more about list management in the next chapter, "Processes.")

> ASK YOURSELF SEVERAL TIMES EVERY DAY, *WHAT'S THE BEST USE OF MY TIME RIGHT NOW?*

Here's something a lot of people miss: Sometimes prioritization overlaps with delegation. As you're thinking about the best use of your time, you also need to be thinking about what you need to be doing as far as directing, managing, and leading your team. You may need to ask yourself, *What do I need to do now so other people can be doing things for me?* For example, you could prioritize phone calls or send emails at the beginning of the day to get others to take action on your behalf. This allows them to prioritize those actions earlier in their own day. Even though the actions they're working on may not be the highest priorities for you personally, you need to start the ball rolling so they can get them done. If you wait until 11:00 a.m. to do that, people may be at lunch, and then they can't start progressing on the things you want done until 1:00 in the afternoon.

Organization

Organization is a huge time-saving tool! Let me give you eight powerful tips for getting better organized:

1. Organize lists, to-dos, and other content by using your memo, tasks, or notes area of your phone. Leverage what is available to you with organizational focus. (We'll talk more about this in chapter four, when we dive into using the phone as one of your most important tools.)

> LEVERAGE WHAT IS AVAILABLE TO YOU WITH ORGANIZATIONAL FOCUS.

2. Double up on tasks. Create an *Elegant Solution* with your actions. (Exercising + reading = time savings.)

3. Listen to audio books or watch videos or snippets from key authorities who are on the web while you're doing something else—even when you're shaving or maybe taking a bath. (Go to https://tonyjeary.com/results-faster-app to get our free RESULTS Faster app.) These are great sources for research and briefings. Make sure you're listening all the time. Be organized so you'll be ready, because if you're not organized, you often won't do it. You'll procrastinate.

> WHENEVER POSSIBLE, BE SO CLEAR AND ORGANIZED ON YOUR TASKS, GOALS, AND OBJECTIVES THAT YOU CAN MAKE ONE EFFORT AND ACCOMPLISH TWO TO FOUR OR MORE ITEMS WITH THAT ONE ACTIVITY.

4. Surround yourself with valuable tools, including a system for keeping things in the briefcase or backpack you carry with you when travelling.

5. Keep projects, files, and other objects to review and study by the phone to work on while waiting on calls. Multitask when at all possible.

6. Develop a "template agenda" for meetings, and then fine-tune it for every meeting.

7. Keep reading materials organized and with you to read while you are waiting in line, getting your car serviced, etc.

8. Be a list freak when it comes to travel (i.e., make checklists for travel plans, your wardrobe, etc.)

Here are some other things you need to evaluate:

Is your desk area productive for you? Is it motivating? Is it clean? Are files and documents easy to access?

How about your backpack? Can you get to pens, pencils, paper clips, rubber bands, files, cords, or anything else you may need so you don't have to waste time looking for them? How about things like throat lozenges? If you need one and you don't have a supply on hand and easily accessible, you would have to stop at a 7-Eleven, which could cost you fifteen minutes. By keeping things organized in your backpack to keep you healthy, energized, hydrated, and on track, you won't have to make last-minute stops, and you can be much more efficient.

> BY KEEPING THINGS ORGANIZED IN YOUR BACKPACK TO KEEP YOU HEALTHY, ENERGIZED, HYDRATED, AND ON TRACK, YOU WON'T HAVE TO MAKE LAST-MINUTE STOPS, AND YOU CAN BE MUCH MORE EFFICIENT.

How about your vehicles? One of the biggest things people miss is keeping a marketing toolbox in their vehicles. Do you have business cards? Brochures about your company? Gifts to give away?

How organized are your home and your garage? The more organized you are in every area of your life, the more time you can save, and the more powerful you can be in getting things done.

Delegation

I want to share with you these powerful tips on delegation I use and share all the time:

1. Trade projects with an associate or colleague whose abilities and gifts fit the project better than yours.

2. Plan follow-up meetings with the people you've delegated to and check the status of the items or events delegated. In the meetings, ensure the delegatees know that the way you do business is to make it **their** responsibility to keep you updated on the progress. (Transfer ownership to the delegatees.)

> TRANSFER OWNERSHIP TO DELEGATEES; MAKE SURE THEY KNOW THAT THE WAY YOU DO BUSINESS IS TO MAKE IT **THEIR** RESPONSIBILITY TO KEEP YOU UPDATED ON THE PROGRESS OF THE DELEGATED ITEMS.

This is the big thing people often miss in delegation. What often happens is, once you delegate something, you find yourself continually asking, "Where are we on that?" If you transfer to the delegatee the responsibility of keeping you apprised, it saves you tons of time. I have my team members send me recaps of what they accomplished every day, which gives them ownership of how things are progressing versus my owning it.

3. Contract outside services or consultants (even consider college students) when no one in-house has the skills to perform the task or everyone is overburdened. This will gain you valuable time, because you won't have to train and retrain people.

4. Give enough detailed feedback on the projects so delegatees will be able to learn and increase their skills for the next project. This will gain you time in the future and is a great practice of a leader.

5. Have others read and prep for you. Have them research, read, summarize, and pull key bullet points so your time can be spent reading only the most relevant information. Highlighting documents or reports will also save minutes. (Smart Reports are a must!)

6. Create a shortcut language (e.g., pp = please print; SOP = standard operating procedure; etc.).

7. Play to your team members' strengths. Know who's good at what, and let them excel by delegating accordingly.

8. Include instructions to the level needed. If none are needed, save yourself time, and don't include any; if more are needed, ensure that you include them.

9. Use a feedback loop to ensure that the delegation moves forward.

10. Appreciate what you want more of (i.e., proactiveness—taking things before you even delegate them).

11. Trust, yet verify.

12. Balance micromanagement. Lead when you need to lead, and manage when you need to manage, depending on who the recipient is. (Note: Leading saves time.)

A couple of years ago, we put together a little passport book called *How to Gain 100 Extra Minutes a Day*, based on my original time-management book of the same name from twenty years ago. In the passport book, we included a list of responsibilities you can delegate to your assistant to save you a ton of time, as well as a list of things your direct reports can take off your plate. The little book contains many other great time-saving ideas, so I encourage you to go to tonyjeary.com and get a copy to read for yourself, and maybe get enough for your entire team.

CHAPTER THREE
PROCESSES

The third phase of our time-management model is Processes. These are powerful trade secrets I've learned through the years and have taught to my high-achieving clients and their companies all over the world to help them leverage their time, and hence maximize their results.

Check this out: Every process we talk about in this chapter can also be labeled as a good habit. For decades, I've worked with and advised the best masters across industries all over the world, and I've come to believe that there are three basic steps to becoming a master at anything.

Step one: You have to be aware of the different levels (good, great, and mastery) and know what level you're operating in.

Step two: You must understand the benefits of living at the mastery level so your "want-to factor" kicks into high gear. Then you are self-inspired and motivated, because you truly understand the wins you can experience by living at this final success level.

Step three: You must execute to the point of habit (in both thinking and doing). Your habits allow you to produce incredible results over and over.

You can reach and live in the mastery level in time management if you make each of these processes a habit.

Daily List Management

I want to emphasize how powerful this time-management secret is. In about half of the over fifty books I've authored, I've stressed the importance of creating, leveraging, and reviewing lists often, and then asking yourself my favorite little question, *What's the best use of my time right now?*

Most people don't have the mental discipline to consistently create a list at the beginning of their day and really master the mentality of processing that list constantly throughout their day. As a result, they fail to get things done in a timely and efficient manner. This process really is a discipline issue, because it takes extreme discipline to make the list before you jump out and start taking action randomly, without prioritizing several times a day.

IF YOU HAVE THE DISCIPLINE TO LIST ALL THE THINGS YOU NEED TO GET DONE AND MENTALLY OWN THEM, AND THEN PRIORITIZE, REVIEW, AND RECHECK YOUR LIST OFTEN DURING THE DAY, YOU'RE GOING TO BE MUCH MORE EFFICIENT WITH YOUR TIME—PERIOD!

If you have the discipline to list all the things you need to get done and mentally own them, and then to prioritize, review, and recheck your list often during the day, you're going to be much more efficient with your time—period! Whether you're making your daily list on your phone, a computer, a flip chart, a legal pad, all the above, or a combination, the benefits to your company or organization and to your life will be astronomical.

Even though managing your daily lists is really a process, the actual list itself is also a powerful tool; as such, we'll go into it in more depth in chapter four.

Team Huddles

HAVING DAILY TEAM HUDDLES IS A POWERFUL PROCESS FOR MANAGING YOUR TIME.

The process of having team huddles is actually more or less a sister to the daily-list process. The idea is to get your team together in a short meeting to discuss everything that will be going on that day (everything on your list). It's a really powerful process for managing your time.

I started personally coaching the president of Walmart (the largest company in the world at that time) in 1996, and I discovered that one of the secrets to Walmart's success is its team huddles. In each of its 4,000 stores (in the United States alone), the management teams do three huddles a day, one for each eight-hour shift. The teams come together for just five or ten minutes to huddle about what's happening that day. And they actually do a little motivational dance at the end of each huddle that really connects everyone as a team. It's called the Walmart Jiggle, and it goes like this: "Give me a W! Give me an A! Give me an L! ..." I think you get the picture.

We also work with a ton of medical and dental practices, where their teams (generally under twenty people) get together and walk through the day—who the patients are, what patients may need special attention or additional time, etc. Some of the doctors I've worked with hold their huddles down to three or four minutes.

In my office, we accumulate all the core things that need to happen each day and put them on one list, and then my team huddles each morning and disseminates those out to five, six, or seven team members. They do that every day so all the team members will have their focus for the day. At the end of the day, they come back and see how they did on the things they needed to get done.

Personally, I prefer not to participate in my team huddles. I choose to have my team members own the responsibility of huddling together and then shooting me any questions they may have or asking for information I can support them with. Some executives want to be part of their team huddles, and others of us (usually from a time perspective) prefer that our teams huddle without us. You just need to decide what works best for you.

Automatic

The more things you can put into play that you don't have to manage, the more time you will save, and the more successful your life can be. It starts with the mindset of being strategic and intentional about putting things into the automatic zone.

You can get more automatic by setting systems in place for things other people can do for you and/or allowing technology to take over some of the tactical things in your life—even by using something as simple as a sprinkler system. One day I realized that my sprinkler system could be expanded to automate another task besides keeping my

THE MORE THINGS YOU CAN PUT INTO PLAY THAT YOU DON'T HAVE TO MANAGE, THE MORE TIME YOU WILL SAVE AND THE MORE SUCCESSFUL YOUR LIFE CAN BE. IT STARTS WITH THE MINDSET OF BEING STRATEGIC AND INTENTIONAL ABOUT PUTTING THINGS INTO THE AUTOMATIC ZONE.

lawn, trees, and shrubs watered. I added a zone to fill my pool, so the pool now gets filled automatically every day.

Making tasks happen automatically frees you up for other, more important things. I put everything I can on automatic (and recommend that you do, as well). Let me give you a few more examples.

- When I get a long-term prescription, I have it mailed to me monthly, and I do the same with my supplements.
- To ensure my van is always ready when my team arrives to drive me somewhere, I set up an automatic system for keeping it gassed up and maintained.
- I even have an automatic system for dry cleaning; when I set my clothes out, they go out to the cleaners. When they come back, I have people who put them in my closet, hung and organized.

Some of those things require a certain level of economics, of course; however, there are a ton of things that cost very little that you can do in your life to make sure things happen automatically. Whether that involves other people doing things for you or using technology, you can really save yourself both time and mental energy by putting things in the automatic zone.

Morning/Evening Rituals

THE MORE YOU CAN MULTITASK (CREATE *ELEGANT SOLUTIONS*) IN YOUR MORNING AND EVENING RITUALS AND MAKE THAT PART OF YOUR PROCESS, THE MORE PRODUCTIVE YOU CAN BE.

From a pure standpoint of time efficiency, the more you can multitask (create *Elegant Solutions*) in your morning and evening rituals and make that part of your process, the more productive you can be.

For example, when I shave in the morning, I often listen to audio recordings. Doing two or three things at once has really become automatic (habitual) for me. I can turn my phone on and knock out a book summary or two or listen to ten minutes of a longer book by the time I finish shaving.

Thirty years ago, I heard an audio recording that said if you studied a subject thirty minutes a day, within a year you would become an expert in that subject. So I thought, *If I study success and results for an hour a day, on average, for the rest of my life, I could become a world-class expert.* I've been doing that now for thirty years! What I do these days in order to really knock that out is listen to audio recordings—often on subjects that align with my values, as well as biographies of successful people—before I go to bed. That's part of my evening ritual. It's the way I go to sleep, and it's the way I maximize my minutes.

What morning and evening rituals can you create to improve your time efficiency?

What's the Best Use of My Time Right Now?
This powerful secret fits into almost every area of our model. We talked about it in chapter two as a major factor in the skill of prioritization, and we emphasized its importance in this chapter as a part of daily-list management. Let me emphasize that asking yourself that question several times a day is powerful. Really, it's *a process to prioritize.* Point made?

CHAPTER FOUR
TOOLS

The final phase of our time-management model is Tools. We're going to talk about five specific tools that will give you the leverage you need to get the extraordinary results you want in managing your time.

The Phone

I believe the phone is one of the most powerful time-saving tools we have available today. I call it a force multiplier —something that dramatically increases (multiplies) the effectiveness of whatever you're doing.

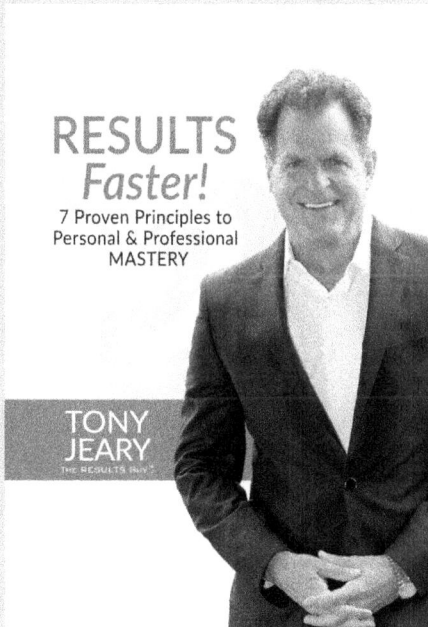

See my RESULTS Faster! book and online video course by the same name at tonyjeary.com/resultsfasterwebinar, in which I talk about the power of force multiplying.

IN TODAY'S WORLD, YOUR PHONE IS ONE OF THE MOST EFFECTIVE FORCE MULTIPLIERS YOU CAN HAVE. UTILIZED CORRECTLY, IT CAN NO DOUBT BE LEVERAGED TO HELP YOU TO GET IMMENSELY BETTER RESULTS, FASTER.

A force multiplier is really about leverage. For example, in today's world your phone is one of the most effective force multipliers you can have. Utilized correctly, it can no doubt be leveraged to help you to get immensely better results, *faster*. I want to take you to a new place in the way you think about your phone—a place where few people go—so you can multiply your time-management capabilities, and hence your results.

Making lists is a key to organization (as we've discussed), and putting your lists on your phone is crucial to making your lists work for you. Consider the impact on your results if you use the notes feature to keep these lists on your phone:

- Your HLAs. Keeping your *High Leverage Activities* on your phone allows you to look at them several times a day to make sure you stay on track with the time you have.
- Your to-do list. You want to be able to look at your to-do list throughout the day, as well, and ask yourself, *What's the best use of my time right now?*
- Your daily performance standards (we'll talk about these later in this chapter)
- Your *Life Team*. Keep an organized list of your *Life Team* members (CPA, attorney, coach, electrician, plumber, etc.) on your phone, including their name, role, and contact information. Having that information on your phone saves a ton of time when you need advice or something done right away.

Be sure to keep your phone organized so you can get to your lists quickly and in good working order—charged, with chargers everywhere—so you can be prepared and ready at all times.

Some people have the skills to use and operate two or three phones to their fullest capacity, and yet most don't. I often carry two or three with me, because different phones have different functions, capabilities, capacities, and qualities. One of the phones I use is a very special Blackberry from France. The keyboard is exceptional for a writer/author like myself. I can get to files quickly, and it has the cut-and-paste feature on it that saves me probably ten to fifteen minutes every day. It just gives me more flexibility and efficiency than I can get on my iPhone. I do love my iPhone, though, and am constantly upgrading it to the latest and greatest. Each phone has its own nuances; so by carrying two or three, I have an almost inexhaustible list of ways my phones can help me save time. I always have backups, and I often use two at the same time.

When new people come on my team, I ask them to put in their phone the top twenty-five people they will be calling most often on my behalf. We have thousands of contacts, and that little technique helps them quickly look up those we call the most—it saves their time, thus saving my time as well.

The phone also gives you leverage with all the time-saving software (apps) there are. You can perform just about any task on your phone now, rather than having to use your computer or take up valuable time going to brick-and-mortar locations.

Are you using your phone to the level you could? Think about how you can maximize it to go to another level.

Accelerator Matrix
One of my favorite tools for helping people I coach get clear on their HLAs is the *Accelerator Matrix*, which we've included on the next page. Once you've identified your HLAs (focus areas) and accelerators (primary actions), you can use this tool to better determine and document what roadblocks you will need to prepare to go through, around, or over. You can see at a glance the things you need to watch for and avoid, which makes it an excellent time-saving tool.

Name/Department/Role: _____   Date:_____

ACCELERATOR MATRIX

Overall Objectives:			
#	**HLAs / Focus Areas**	**Accelerators (Primary Actions)**	**Roadblocks to Bust**
1.			
2.			
3.			
4.			
5.			
6.			
7.			

Lists

I'm such a huge proponent of making lists to help you save major amounts of time that I wanted to include it again here in the "Tools" chapter. It is, in fact, one of the most powerful tools you can use to move your results needle forward. Lists allow you to free up your mind so you can get things done. Instead of completing a task and then hovering around for a few minutes before deciding what to do next, you can just open up your phone and see what your next priority item is and then knock it out quickly.

There's no one-size-fits-all way to keep lists. I'm a firm believer in putting your lists on your phone, on your computer, and anywhere else you can see them easily—even on a board in your office. The idea, of course, is the more you use lists as a tool and the more often you look at them, the more they will help you get the right things done—faster.

Use multiple lists. Remember, the more things you write down, the more it frees up your mind. Yes, it may take some effort; and, yes, you might not get something else done as quickly because you're taking the time to make a list. Yet, by taking those few minutes, you're going to be more powerful with your time, and you're going to get the right things done. Seeing all the X's in the boxes next to the items on your to-do list as you move through your day is a real motivator!

In our office, we create a master list of everything that's going on. Then we have a daily to-do list of the priority items we need to stay on top of. We may have sublists for some projects, such as meetings with new or potential clients. Then there are other lists. For example, when I meet with someone, I like to have a bulleted list of who they are and what they're about. This allows me to be thoroughly prepared before I talk to them. And I find it extremely powerful to sometimes have my team prepare a competitive comparison list before I talk to a client so I can see who their competitors are and discover a little about each one. I also recommend keeping lists of your *Life Team* members and your *People of Influence* (POI) on your phone.

Standards

Most people have never taken the time to document standards for themselves and/or their organizations. They may say they have them, yet few have documented them. Standards are an essential time-management tool. Let me explain.

As you know by now, I've worked with some of the brightest people in the world—people who have run extremely successful enterprises of all different kinds. Those leaders want the people below them in their organization to understand how they think. That includes anyone who joins their team, regardless of the size of the company. For the most part, leaders at the top have gone through many experiences and solved a multitude of problems, and they have developed personal systems and processes that work. They want and often expect others to simply grab onto their thinking. Yet sometimes it takes weeks, months, and even years for that to happen—*unless* they have documented standards and have taken the time to say, "If you're going to play on my team, these are the standards you'll need to live by."

The super performers actually integrate their written guidelines or standards into their culture. They take the time to document their standards, post them, and teach them, so when new people are onboarded, it's an easy matter of saying, "Here are our standards." New hires are not left to wonder for weeks or months how things work or what's important. They are shown the standards right up front so they can produce at a higher level, and everyone wins.

SUPER PERFORMERS ACTUALLY HAVE THEIR WRITTEN STANDARDS BECOME PART OF THEIR CULTURE.

I believe both personal and professional standards are important. I have personal standards—things I want to do every day—and professional standards for my team.

Personal standards set the stage for minimal distractions, guide your decisions, and help you say "no" more often so you can get rid of *Low-Leverage Activities.*

Let me share with you my twelve personal standards—twelve specific things I do every day:

1. Start each morning by praying for wisdom.

2. Do team huddles or stimulate huddles for my team. I believe incredible synergy comes from doing team huddles.

3. Glance at my new business opportunities to keep them fresh in my mind. My relationship manager sends me an email every morning, and I look at it and think about the opportunities that are ahead of me. I want to keep those fresh in my mind every day so I have them down tight.

4. Determine my top priorities for the day or the week. As I mentioned, we have a master to-do list that we look at every day and determine the top priorities. I look at the master list throughout the day to see what my personal priorities are, because I want to make sure I'm doing the things that are at the top of my list. At the end of the day, I want to know that I got the most important things done—not that I just got a ton of things done.

5. Touch my family and my team members inspirationally in some way.

6. Compliment and communicate appreciation for those around me. People crave appreciation.

7. Stretch, flex, and breathe with both confidence and gratitude. I want to keep my body healthy, and I want to appreciate everything I have. Gratitude makes me a better person.

8. Organize and rationalize to keep things clean. (Be a river, not a reservoir.) If you were to look at my closets, you would see that they're clean. And the same with my car. I'm constantly giving things away to get them out of my life and keep things clean and organized.

9. Visualize my own goals (short- and long-term) with focus and clarity. What you have real clarity about and focus on is what you execute. I visualize everything, and I study my vision board every day.

VISUALIZE YOUR GOALS WITH FOCUS AND CLARITY. WHAT YOU HAVE REAL CLARITY ABOUT AND FOCUS ON IS WHAT YOU EXECUTE.

10. Model exceptional behavior, including enjoying life. I encourage you to stop and enjoy the moment. If you have sunshine, enjoy it. If you have

rain, find ways to enjoy the rain. I want to love and enjoy every single day of my life. How about you?

11. Eat healthy. I have my team make sure nothing gets in front of me that's not healthy, because I get tempted just like everyone else does. I don't want unhealthy food in my pantries or refrigerators. I want every food item I see to be healthy.

12. Doing favors for those who are a part of my life. I make giving gifts an important part of my life. I handwrite notes and send them to hundreds of people a year; I email out best ideas; and when I find videos I think are valuable, I send those links to people. I'm constantly doing favors for others so I can help them be their best.

Professional standards could be just for you and those you might delegate to, or they could be for those you recruit to your team or organization. When I work with executives, I push them to get clear on their professional standards.

We have my professional standards posted in every room in my office, and I encourage you to do the same. I also have my team members include them in the very first in-person interview when they're recruiting people for our firm. They tell the people being interviewed that if we make them an offer, they need to know that these standards are solid expectations of how we operate, and they need to make sure they can live with them. Here are my professional standards:

1. **Save Tony's Time,** keeping him in front of and serving our clients.

2. **Kaizen** means constant improvement for all team members—including on-going COEs, personal SWOTs, and MOLO refinements.

3. Keep everything clean and **Organized**. This adds to our brand and makes us always ready.

4. Constant **List making** ensures prioritizing, accountability, and execution of faster results (including CSFs).

5. Over-**Communicate** and calculate. This helps ensure efforts are maximized. Avoid absolutes—words like "never," "always," and "can't" (because all things are possible).

6. **Focus** efforts on new flow of business/revenue. Daily priorities include pipeline management, SOW development, and processing receivables. Remember, cash is king!

7. Do *Favors in Advance* (**FIA**)—sharing, giving, and helping others win.

8. **Do things now**! Operate with a mindset of quick action and speed to completion, while using *Production Before Perfection*—manage procrastination.

9. Be **Proactive** in everything (think ahead, prep ahead, do ahead, invoice ahead, deliver ahead, and exceed expectations all around—internally and externally).

10. Employ the **Team** approach—overlap, cross-support, encourage, leverage each other's expertise, and together keep all eyes on getting things done and completed, with RESULTS produced hourly, daily, and weekly.

At the very foundation of all of my standards, both personal and professional, is my mantra: Give value and do more than is expected. It overarches everything I do personally and all that both my team and I do professionally. You might consider adopting that as a standard for yourself.

Marty B's is a restaurant in Bartonville, Texas, that gives diners a unique experience with their "live music, welcoming modern ranch atmosphere, delicious Texas specialties, and community fire pits for smores and storytelling." The owner is my friend and client, and he recently shared with me his company's standards, which he created after I shared the idea at Biz Owners Ed (a nonprofit devoted to mentoring). I love it when people take action.

TEN
COMMANDMENTS
TO AMAZING!
MARTY-B's

1 HOSPITALITY
Warm welcome, genuine hi's and goodbyes and a sincere thank you. Use Yes ma'am, no ma'am, yes sir, and no sir when talking with guests.

2 PERSONAL GROOMING
Take pride in your appearance: smiles, hair, nails, uniform, and facial care.

3 TRAINING
Know the menu and steps of service. Be Confident! When asking how the guest enjoyed the food use words like Amazing! Fantastic! Excellent! Perfect! Awesome! Etc.

4 SAFETY
Watch for food or water on floors, sharp objects, broken plates or glassware, and the safety of our little friends and guests. Keep hot food hot, cold food cold.

5 SPEED / WORK ETHIC
Move with a sense of urgency. Be quick but don't hurry.

6 ACCURACY
Listen intently to guests to ensure we get the order correct. Repeat order back to guest.

7 TEAMWORK
Support your teammates at any and all times. Pre-bussing, drink refills, running food, re-stocking etc.

8 PUNCTUALITY
Arrive on time and prepared to work.

9 CLEANLINESS
IMMACULATE is the goal.

10 FUN!
Have fun with the guest. Remember this is more than a restaurant. It is an experience.

Goal-Setting Tool Box

We talked in chapter one about the importance of knowing your values, and we provided a list of sixty values so you could identify those that best define what means the most to you. When people come into my private studio, I have a deck of cards with those sixty values on them, and I have them do a "values tournament" similar to the exercise we suggested you do in chapter one. We also included in that chapter another goal-setting tool called the Values Goals Matrix, which allows you to ensure alignment among your values, HLAs, and goals, both personally and professionally.

Another helpful tool we have is a model (shown below) that shows the relationship between values, purpose, dreams and goals, and actions. You start by getting clear on your values. Then if you like, you can design a purpose statement, which really helps you gain clarity. Most people skip this step. Then you need to set your goals, making sure they align with your values and your purpose. From there, you need to identify your actions that will turn your goals into reality.

I believe that if you integrate these tools into your daily life, you'll be surprised—even shocked—at the amount of time you'll gain. This will allow you to focus on the important steps you must take to get the results you want.

NOTES

_____

_____

_____

_____

_____

_____

_____

_____

_____

_____

_____

_____

_____

_____

_____

_____

_____

_____

_____

_____

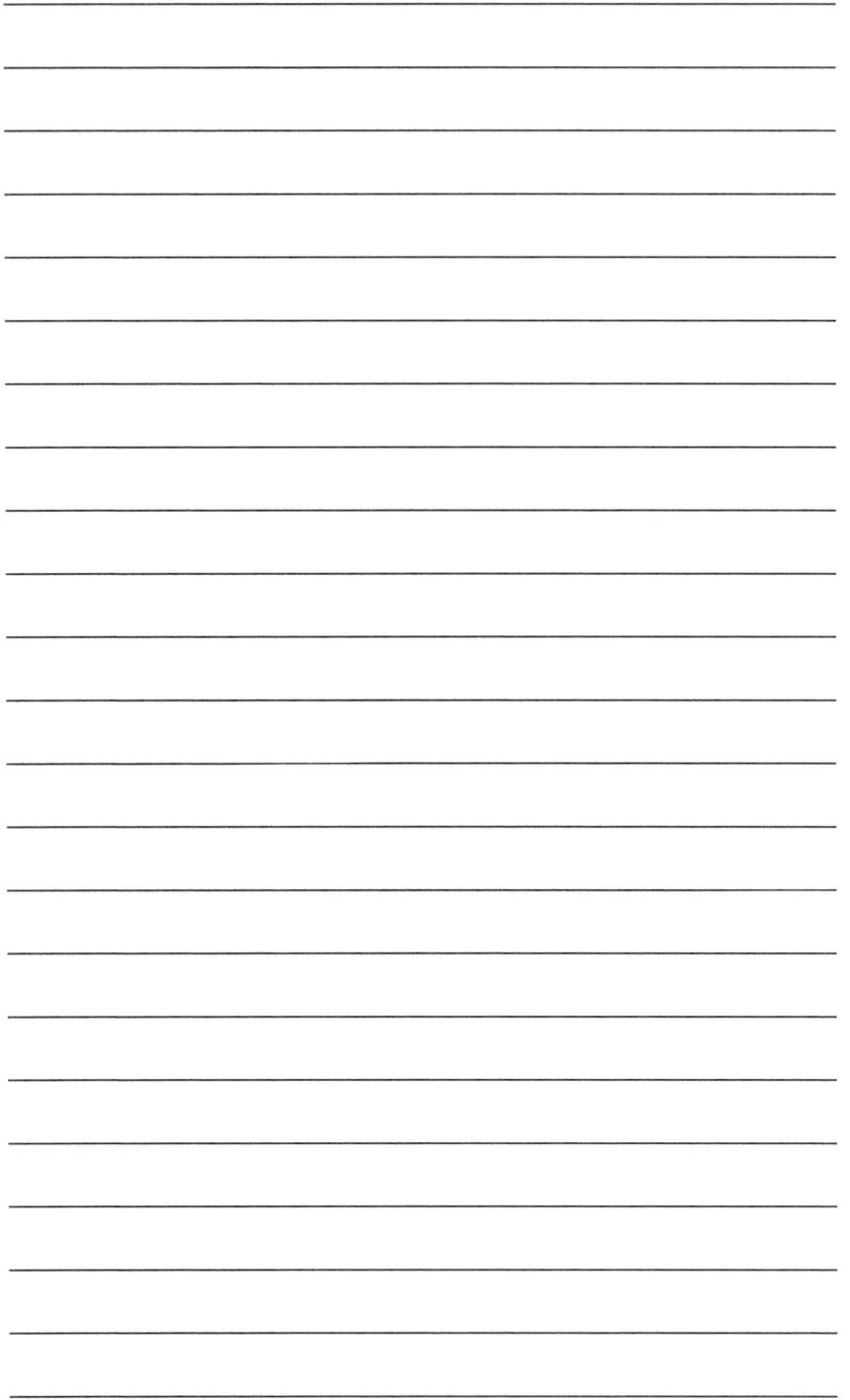

CONCLUSION

Getting the right results faster for individuals and organizations is what I've dedicated my professional life to, and I believe that being strategic about your time is half the battle.

Remember, my tagline is "Change your thinking, change your results." (Search for "Tony Jeary on Change Your Thinking, Change Your Results" and watch the short video.) Here's how I think that applies here:

- Once you become aware of and understand fundamental truths such as maintaining an "investing vs. spending" mindset about time, tying your actions into your values, and investing time to think, then you've laid a solid foundation for strategic change.
- Next when you master time-management skills like saying "no" strategically (watch my "Tony Jeary on Saying No" video, as well), holding more efficient meetings, prioritizing, delegating, and organizing, I would bet you've already made giant strides toward changing your results.
- Implementing powerful processes like list management, team huddles, and moving things to automatic, and then adding tools like maximizing the use of your phone, creating standards for yourself and your organization, and employing our goal-setting tools can help you nail down the results you're looking for.

What are you waiting for? Go for it!

About the Author

When many of the world's top achievers seek a strategic expert to help them accelerate their results, they are eventually drawn to Tony Jeary. Tony is the authority on RESULTS and has committed his career to studying and helping others think better and achieve more. If you want to better your life, your career, your organization, and your results, you need to know Tony.

Tony was raised by entrepreneurial parents and grandparents who thrived on identifying and pursuing new opportunities to serve others. His father taught him the powerful principle that has driven Tony's professional and personal life: "Always give more than is expected." Exceeding expectations is the common thread that every Tony Jeary client experiences firsthand. Tony has advised people around the world (in some fifty countries) for over thirty years. He has published more than four dozen books, now in over a dozen languages. And he has worked with CEOs from many of the Fortune 500 companies and entrepreneurial families from the Forbes Richest 400. Tony has been described as a "gifted encourager" who facilitates positive outcomes for others. His list of personal and professional relationships approaches 40,000 people, whom he connects with and nourishes out of his sincere interest and desire for shared success.

Tony's clients include individuals and organizations who are involved globally. He personally coaches the presidents of organizations like Ford, Walmart, Samsung, TGI Fridays, New York Life, Firestone, Sam's Club, and many more.

Tony has personal experience with both success and failure. He made and lost millions before he reached the age of thirty. That early experience with failure propelled him to help others live smart, live on purpose, and be their very best. Today he walks the talk and practices the distinctions that characterize success, both personally and professionally, sharing daily and encouraging others to think strategically about everything. He is blessed with a terrific marriage of over twenty-five years, two great daughters (both of whom he has coauthored books with), and one fantastic son-in-law. Tony currently lives and works on his estate in the Dallas/Fort Worth area where his private RESULTS Studio is located. For more information, contact his company at *info@tonyjeary.com.*

WHAT TONY JEARY INTERNATIONAL CAN DO FOR YOU

Results Coaching

Advice Matters, if it's the right advice. Having coached the world's top CEOs; published hundreds of books, videos, and courses; and advised clients in virtually every industry, across six continents, and at every stage of growth, Tony has positioned himself with a unique track record to take serious high achievers to a whole new level of results. He carefully selects a few clients to coach each year and is devoted to seeing those clients achieve extraordinary success.

Interactive Keynotes

Tony not only energizes, entertains, and educates; he also orchestrates his team to work strategically and smartly with external event teams to make his performance plus the entire experience a super win. An hour with Tony often changes people's lives forever and impacts an organization's results immediately. He delivers high value with a smart fun factor, and he openly shares best practices that both teams and people can really use.

Strategic Acceleration Facilitation Planning

Tony can do in a single day what takes others days and even weeks to accomplish. He encourages people to think strategically and has refined his process to be so powerful, that clients from all over the world travel miles to arrive at his RESULTS Center. Here, they gain a better understanding of what it means to have clarity and focus, and they improve their ability to synergistically execute. Tony has at his fingertips three decades of best practices, processes, and tools for accelerating dramatic, sustained results in any organization.

Collaborative Relationships

TJI selectively partners with a handful of select organizations in an annual collaborative arrangement where we pour our knowledge and wisdom into the top leader(s) and their entire organization(s) and help build a super-charged, motivated, and engaged High-Performing Team We align with top entrepreneurs and C-Level management's vision and become an extension of them. The bottom line is, we help: Clarify vision and focus on what matters most—High Leverage Activities (HLAs)—so people and entire organizations can execute and get the right results faster.

"Change your thinking change your results; it's that simple."
—Tony Jeary

TONYJEARY.COM
JOIN US ON THE
RESULTS FASTER! APP

We are excited to share with you the Results Faster! app, which is available on the web for all devices. To get started, go to https:// tonyjeary. ihubapp.org and click the Login button in the top right corner. If this is your first time logging in, click on "Register." Once registered, you then have instant access to our Gold Level channels, which include our most popular, most requested resources! Use the left-hand menu to view the channel numbers. Join any channels that are of interest to you, and the content will populate right on the home page of your Results Faster! app.

www.ingramcontent.com/pod-product-compliance
Lightning Source LLC
Chambersburg PA
CBHW071609200326
41519CB00021BB/6930